Basic Kuna

Kuna-Spanish-English

Dictionary

&

Words and Phrases

Basic Kuna:
Kuna-Spanish -English Dictionary
Words and Phrases

Edited by Timothy P. Banse

ISBN: 978-0-934523-13-4 PRINT
ISBN: 978-0-934523-14-1 E-book

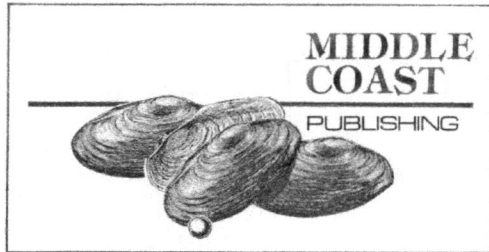

MIDDLE
COAST
PUBLISHING

DEDICATION

This book is dedicated to Abi Sua, the infant child born on the island of *Nargana* (circa 1985) of sailor parents, an English father from the Channel Islands and Brazilian mother from *Fuertalaza, Brasil,* who sought shelter from a storm at sea.

WORDS AND PHRASES

COLORS OF THE RAINBOW

Black - Sichid
Blue -Arrad
Brown -Cuturguagua
Green - Aradgua
Orange - Gordikit
Pink - Kisigua
Red - Ginnid
White - Sipuwad
Yellow - Gorogwa

WHO, WHAT, WHEN and WHERE

Where? - Biali
When? - Sanagua
Why? - Ibigala
What?- Ibua
Who? - Toagua
How? - Igui
How much? - Igui merge

NUMBERS

One - Wargwen
Two - Warbo
Three - Warba
Four - Wapakke
Five - Walattale

Six   - Walanergwa
Seven - Walakugle
Eight - Walapaabak
Nine - Walabakkebak
Ten - Waarme
Twenty   - Warturwuen
Hundred - Walatuambe

FAMILY RELATIONSHIPS

Father   - baba
Mother - nana
Husband - suit
Wife - ome
Son An - machi
Daughter - an buna
Brother - ia
Sister - bunor
Grandfather - dada
Grandmother - muu
Grandchild - wagwa

COMMON PHRASES

I don't have any money - Mani sate
I don't know - An wichuli
Where are you going? - Bia be nae
How do you say...? - Igi soilegue

Hello   - Te gui te
How are you?- Be nuedi
I am fine- An nuedi
Everything is good -   Nua gambi
I don't understand-   An aku be itogue
I need to use the bathroom - An servicio an dice navie

I am hungry   - An aku
Se you later - Cuzar maloe
I am thirsty - An ti ko
See you tomorrow- Pane malo
What time is it? - Igi uachi gusa
Do you want to play?   - Be todo bie
Where are you from?   - Be bia liti
What is your name? - Igi be nuga
My name is - An nuga
Thank you -   Nuegambi
You are welcome - Nuedi
The food is delicious - Mas yer culege

Good morning - Nuedi
Good night - Nuedi
Good aftermoon - Nuedi
Goodbye - tequimalo
How are you?- Be nuedi
Nice to meet you - An yer itoge conocer be sai
I don't speak kuna - An dule calla suimai suli
Do you speak Spanish - Be español sunmake
Good luck - Nue gambi be maloi

I don't have any money - Mani sate
I don't know - An wichuli
Where are you going - Bia be nae
How do you say. . . ?   - Igi soilegue

Yes -Elle
No -Suli
Thanks -Dot Nuet
Please -Uis anga saet
Ok -Nued gudii o
Good -Nabir, nuedi
Welcome -Nuegambi use be noniki

Hello -Na
How are you? -Bede nued guddi?
Fine, thank you. And you? -An nuedi. Bedina?
Fine -Nuedi

What is your name? -Igi be nuga?
My name is Timothy -An nuga Timothy
Nice to meet you -An yeel itoe
Where are you from? -Be bia lidi?
I am from -An . . . ginedi.

I'm hungry -An uku itoe
I'm thirsty -An gobie
I'm cold -An dambe itoe
I'm warm -An uerba itoe
I'm sleepy -An nue gapie
I'm happy -An yee ito dii
Let's go -Anmar nae

How much does this cost? -Que mani?
I want to buy it -An bag bie

Do you speak English? -Be sumake merki galla?
Come here -Uesik dage
Look at that -Dake
Speak slowly please -Uis binna sunmake
I don't understand -Aku ittoe

I'm sorry -An oakue
Good bye -Degi malo
Good luck -Nuedgine, nuegan bi
I'll see you tomorrow -An banedes

PRONOUNS

I / Me	An
You	Be
He / She	Wae
We	Anmar
They	Wer

Dictionary

Kuna	Spanish	English
	A	
Abeigei	querer	to want
Abya Yala	las Americas	the Americas, literally, saved land
Acua		rocks
Acua bisiki	arrecifes	coral reefs
Acuadop		rock island
Acualele (acuanusa)	piedra suave del río	smooth river rock, sometimes attributed with healing powers
Achuagua	embrazar	hug
Akwei	cuidar	to care for
Alei	sonrisa	smile

Ama	tia	aunt
Amagutza	cayer	to fall
Ampokamala	dormir	to sleep
An	mío	mine
Andup	mi isla	my island
Anmimmi	mi hijo	my child
Anai	amigo	friend
Ani	yo	I/me
Angi	langostino	crawfish
Anmar	nosotros	we
Anugaden	Me llamo	My name is
Arkar	representante del gobierno	spokesperson for the chief
Arson		ladder
Asu	nariz	nose

	B	
Baba	papa, padre (dios)	father (often God)
Bab Dummad	gran padre, creador	
Bab Igala	sendero de nuestro señor	The Road of God, the path of creation itself.
Bab Tummat	dios masculino	male god
Bei	tu/usted	you
Bei igi birga nika?	¿cuantos años tiene usted?	How old are you?
Beiyabenega?	¿de donde eres?	Where are you from?
Beikeniginika?	¿como se llama?	What's your name?
Bia natei?	Dondé esta?	Where is it?
Bipi	pequeño	small
-- Dupbipi	isleta	small island
-- Negabipi	casita	small house

8

-bo	ambos	Both. This suffix is added to the second of two subjects, for instance, "Be nika anai guarbo, Judy Timbo," which means, "You have two friends, both Judy and Tim." A common way to form: and.
Boei	ceño	frown
Boni	enfermadad	illness
Birya	tormenta, lugar de espiritos malos	storm, tornado, home of evil spirits
Builatokei	pobrecito	oh, you poor thing you
Buñulogwa	niño	medium-sized child
Burba	alma, forteleza, vigor, sentido	soul, feeling

	C	
Capi	café	coffee
Cagan	césped	grass
Carta Organica	Carta Organica	Kuna Yala constitution
Chiagua	cacao	cocoa
Chicha	bebida alcoholica de maiz	an alcoholic drink made of fermented corn Chicha also refers to monthly four-day celebrations.
Chili	negro	black
Chuchu	mariposa	butterfly
Coco loco		coconut milk with rum
Congresos		town meeting
Coroguat	amarillo	yellow

	D	
Dada/Baba	padre, abuelo	father, grandfather
Daisa	vi	I saw
Datoibei	sol	sun
Deimar	mar	sea
Dien	lagarto	crocodile, alligator
Digei	sembrar	to plant
Diguargit	verde	green
Diguarr	río	river
Dinit	rojo	red
Domumakei	nadar	to swim
Dule (Tulei)	la gente, persona	the people
Dulemola	ropa de la gente	The "people's clothes," or traditional clothing of the Kuna people.
Duleigaya	idioma	Cuna language
Dulup	langosta	lobster
Dumat	grande	big
Dupdumat	isla grande	big island
Dupu	isla	island

	E	
Eduei	cerrado	closed
Eiki	abierto	open
Eimi	hoy	today
Eiomei	esposa	wife
Eiyei	si	yes
Erragon		a kuna god
Escubiyei	loco	crazy
Esnou		machete
Esui	esposo	husband

	G	
Galu	hogar de los espiritus	home of the spirits
Ganil	pollo	chicken
Gerdaileigei	hermosa	beautiful
Gono	dedo	finger, toe
Goukim	hombros	shoulders
Guadigip	morada, azul	blue, purple
Guage	corazón	heart
Gundeileibi	ahogar	to drown
Guneimasi	comer	to eat

I

Ibia	ojo	eye
Ibia guarbo	ojos	eyes
Ico Inna		feast marking puberty or wedding.
Igala	sendero, camino	road, path
Imasubalei	tatuaje	tattoo
Ina	medicina	natural medicinal plants, traditional medicine in general
Ibelelekana	heroes culturales	The family of deities
Inaduled	doctor botánico	Kuna doctor, any type of botanist
Ipa	nube	cloud
Ipe	sol	sun
Itiguin	aqui	here
Iyagua	señora	woman

K

Kaa	un chile picante	hot pepper
Katchi	hamaca	hammock
Kaka	boca	mouth
Kalu	tierra sagrada	sacred ground
Kami remo	remo	oar
Kanaletei	remar	to row
Kilu	tio	uncle
Kilu Ulusui Dios de Cocodrilios	Uncle Long Canoe	The crocodile god of the underworld.
Kiplu	aguila	hawk
Koibir	coco	coconut
Koirgua	papaya	papaya
Korokwa	maduro	ripe
Koskun Kalu	Congreso Kuna	Yala Congress of Kuna Yala
Koyei	muñeca	doll
Kukwei	volar	to fly
Kukunai	volar en avion	to fly in a plane
Kuna	persona/pueblo	person/people
Kuna Yala		Kuna territory
Kunei	comer	eat
Kunu	plastico	plastic
Kurgen	sombrero, gorro	hat

Kwalu	papa dulce	sweet potato
Kwallu	grasa	grease
Kwento	cuento	story

	M	
Macharit	hombre	man
Machi	niño	boy
Madu	pan	bread
Magei	maquilarse	to put on makeup
Mani	plata	silver
Marganai	relâmpagos	lightning
Marto		Hammer
Mergi	turista	gringo tourist
Merginega	Estados Unidos	House of the Americans
Mimmi	niño, hijo	child
Misi	gato	cat
Mo	calabasas	squash
Moguir	cielo	sky
Mola	ropa, camisa	shirt of piece of lothing, but also reverse applique art form.

Mora	tela	cloth
Morlgo	herida	wound
Morrbep	caracol	snail, conch
Mulatupo	Archipelago San Blas	San Blas Islands
Mulmakei	persona que hace molas	mola maker
Muu oceano,	abuela anciana	grandmother, elder female

N

Nadamakei	escribir	to write
Nadapi	se fue	to have left
Omei nadapi	ella se fue	the woman left
Naga	pie	foot
Namakei	cantar	sing
Nana	madre	mother
Nali	tiburon	shark
Napa	tierra firma	the mainland
Napguana	Madre Tierra	Mother Earth
Narascam	naranjo	orange
Natei	fue	he or she, went
Necheglaun	mundo	world
Neg Kunas	tierra	earth

Neka	casa, lugar	house, place
Negadumat	casa grande	big house
Negusmatar		roof
Neg seged	Selva primaria	
Nei maked		paint
Nei tikar		wall
Nei turwied		broom
Nele		shaman, wise one
nelegan		
Ni	luna	moon
Nia malo	el diablo	Satan, evil, heathen devil weed marijuana
Nika	tener	to have
Nisqua	estrella	star
Nono	cara, rostro	face
Nuba	estomago	stomach
Nuchu		fetish, typically a small, carved wooden doll.
Nuga	nombre	name
Nuwedi	bueno	catch-all phrase meaning

		Good Morning and Thank You, the same word for both. Also used for Hello and Goodbye.
Nuweigambi	mucho gusto	nice to meet you

O

Obei	playa	beach
Ogob	coco (cocos nucifera)	coconut
Olo or oro		gold necklace
Olowaili	Diosa de Paz	goddess of peace
Olu	gallo	rooster
Olua	arretes	earrings
Ome	mujer	woman
Opi	nadar	to swim
Osi	piña	pineapple
Ornasi	uñas	fingernails
Orr	barco	boat (no sail)
Orrgo		wood
Oua	pez, pescado	fish

P

Panaba	muy lejos	very far away
Panei	mañana	tomorrow
Paneimalo	hasta la mañana	until tomorrow, good night
Pap kalimpapa	cielo	father's place (heaven)
Po	llorar	to cry
Poni		evil spirit
Punagua		

S

Sagir burua	Vientos del Rio Chagres	Rio Chagres winds
Sahila	cacique, jefe	spiritual or political leader
Sapi	árbol	tree
Sapudei	falda	skirt
Sanda	chancletas, sandales	sandals
Saqua	mano, brazo	hand, arm
Satei	no	no
Sia	sobrino	niece/nephew

Sirro	ombligo	navel, belly button
Siagua	cocoa	chocolate
Siglei	ayer	yesterday
Sigue	sientate	have a seat
Sika	barba, bigote	beard, mustache
Siligwia	pelo	hair
Skungit		lobster
So	fuego	fire
Soi	pescar	to fish
Suga	cangrejo	crab
Suli	no	no
Suna	verdad	truth

T

Tabu	barracuda	barracuda
Takei	ver	to see
Takei malo	adios	goodbye
Tadarguanet	donde puesto del sol	where the sun sets
Tii	agua	water
Tule	hombre	man
Tulemola		kuna clothing

Tumbi	comer	to eat
Tupbak	ballena	whale
Tutu	suelo	floor

	U	
Ua	pez	fish
Uaga	extranjero	foreigner
Uakad	puerto	door
Uaymadun	variedad de guineo	banana
Ukubu	arena	sand
Uku sued		shovel
Unolugwa	niña/o	child
Ulu	canoa	dugout canoe
Unmorr	barco a vela	sailboat
Urgo		wood
Urgo siked		saw
Urrba	nieto, hermano	grandchild, younger sibling
Urrbali	bajo	under

	V	
Vini	conejo	rabbit

	W	
Wa	humo	smoke
Waga	extranjero	foreigner, outsider, non-Kuna, including most Panamanians
Wagalumala	beso	a kiss
Wagaluei	besar	to kiss
Warkwen	solo	only, alone
Weechup	una fruta morada	a small, purple fruit
Wini	abalorios	beads or anything made from beads
Winibaizna		beaded armbands
Wisi	saber	to know
Wei	el or ella	he or she
Weimar	ellos	they or them
Wood	maduro	urgo

Y

Yala	montaña	mountain
Yala burua	vientos del Sur, de las montañas	South wind
Yalatela	pez	fish
Yeiolo	hermano mayor	an older sibling
Yo	codo	elbow
Yokorr	rodilla	knee
Yoor burua	vientos alisisos del Norte	North winds

www.ingramcontent.com/pod-product-compliance
Lightning Source LLC
Chambersburg PA
CBHW060606030426
42337CB00019B/3637